World of Wonder
DINOSAURS

Roar!

SALARIYA

Published in Great Britain
in 2007 by Book House,
an imprint of
**The Salariya Book
Company Ltd**
25 Marlborough Place,
Brighton BN1 1UB

Editor: Rob Walker

Author: David Stewart has
written many non-fiction books
for young children. He lives in
Brighton with his wife and son.

Artist: Nick Hewetson studied
illustration at Eastbourne
College of Art and has since
illustrated a wide variety of
children's books.

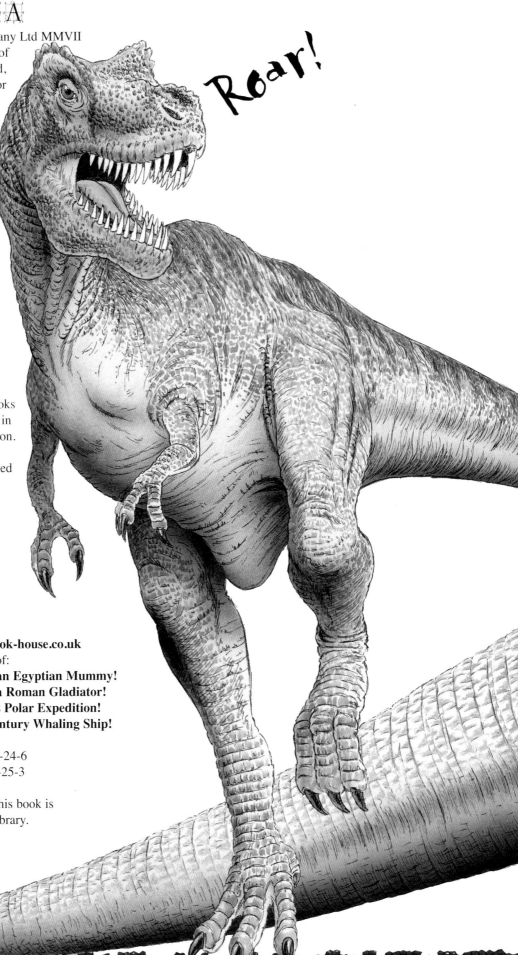

Roar!

Visit our website at **www.book-house.co.uk**
for **free** electronic versions of:
You Wouldn't Want to be an Egyptian Mummy!
You Wouldn't Want to be a Roman Gladiator!
Avoid Joining Shackleton's Polar Expedition!
Avoid Sailing on a 19th-Century Whaling Ship!

HB ISBN-13: 978-1-905638-24-6
PB ISBN-13: 978-1-905638-25-3

A CIP catalogue record for this book is
available from the British Library.

Printed and bound in China.
Printed on paper from
sustainable sources.

World of Wonder
Dinosaurs

Written by

David Stewart

Illustrated by

Nick Hewetson

Contents

What were dinosaurs?

Dinosaurs were reptiles, a type of animal with scaly skin. Reptiles that live now include lizards, snakes and crocodiles. There were many different kinds of dinosaurs: plant-eaters and meat-eaters, some tiny, some huge.

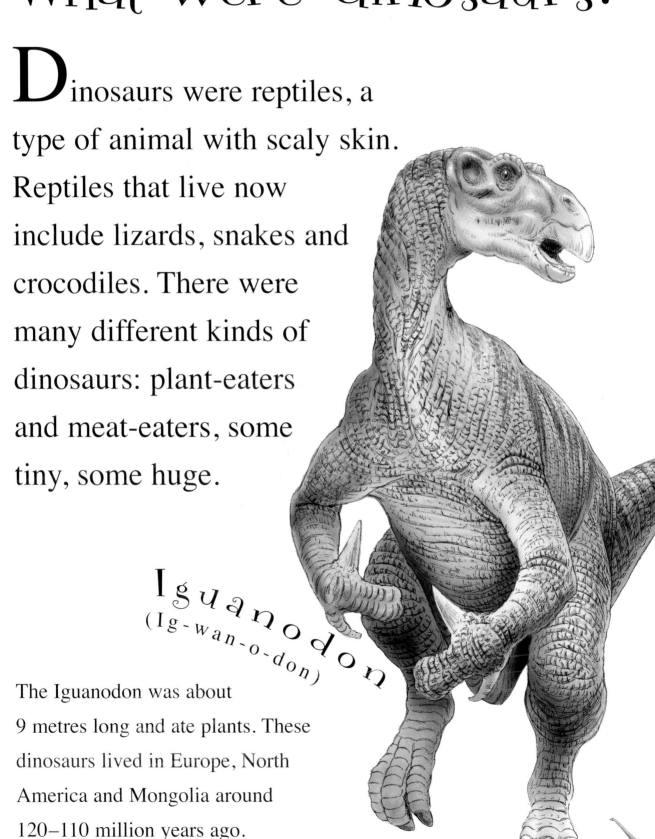

Iguanodon
(Ig-wan-o-don)

The Iguanodon was about 9 metres long and ate plants. These dinosaurs lived in Europe, North America and Mongolia around 120–110 million years ago.

When did dinosaurs live?

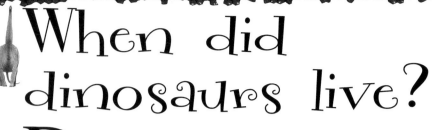

Dinosaurs lived between about 230 million and 65 million years ago. This huge span of time is called the Mesozoic Era.

Did other animals live in the Mesozoic Era?

Yes! Many different animals, including insects, lizards, crocodiles, birds, furry mammals and fish lived at this time, too – but no people.

Grrr!

Scale

The Eoraptor was a one-metre-long meat-eater. These dinosaurs lived in South America.

E o r a p t o r
(Ee-oh-rap-tor)

True or False?

There were more than 700 different kinds of dinosaurs.

Answers on page 31

L a g o s u c h u s
(Lag-oh-soo-cus)

Lagosuchus was a 30-centimetre-long insect-eating dinosaur living in South America 250 million years ago.

Scale

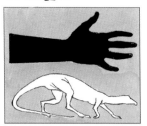

What did dinosaurs eat?

Like most creatures living today, dinosaurs were either meat-eaters or plant-eaters. Plant-eating animals are called **herbivores**.

True or False?

Tyrannosaurus rex had saw-edged teeth.

Answers on page 31

Dinosaurs like Stegosaurus may have swallowed stones to help grind food to a paste in their stomachs. Scientists call these stones **gastroliths**.

Stegosaurus
(steg-oh-sore-us)

Stegosaurus was a herbivore that lived in the **Jurassic** period in North America.

Scale

This shows the size of a Stegosaurus beside a man.

The Stegosaurus had a brain the size of a walnut.

9

Did dinosaurs eat each other?

Yes, huge meat-eating dinosaurs did hunt other dinosaurs. Meat-eating animals are called **carnivores**. Animals that eat plants and meat are called **omnivores**.

Tyrannosaurus rex

(Tie-ran-oh-sore-us rex)

What was the biggest meat-eater?

Tyrannosaurus rex may have been the biggest meat-eater that ever walked on Earth. It hunted other dinosaurs, using its powerful back legs to chase and attack its prey.

True or False?

The word 'dinosaur' is Greek for 'terrible lizard'.

Answers on page 31

10

Tyrannosaurus rex had strong jaws and teeth which ripped chunks of flesh from its victims.

Grrr!

Tyrannosaurus rex means 'king tyrant lizard'. It grew to be about 14 metres long and 5 metres tall.

Scale

Did dinosaurs lay eggs?

Many **fossilised** dinosaur eggs have been found. Some dinosaurs laid eggs just like birds and reptiles do today – they simply scooped out a hole in the ground for their nests.

Oviraptor
(Ov-i-rap-tor)

Oviraptor eggs have been found in southern Mongolia.

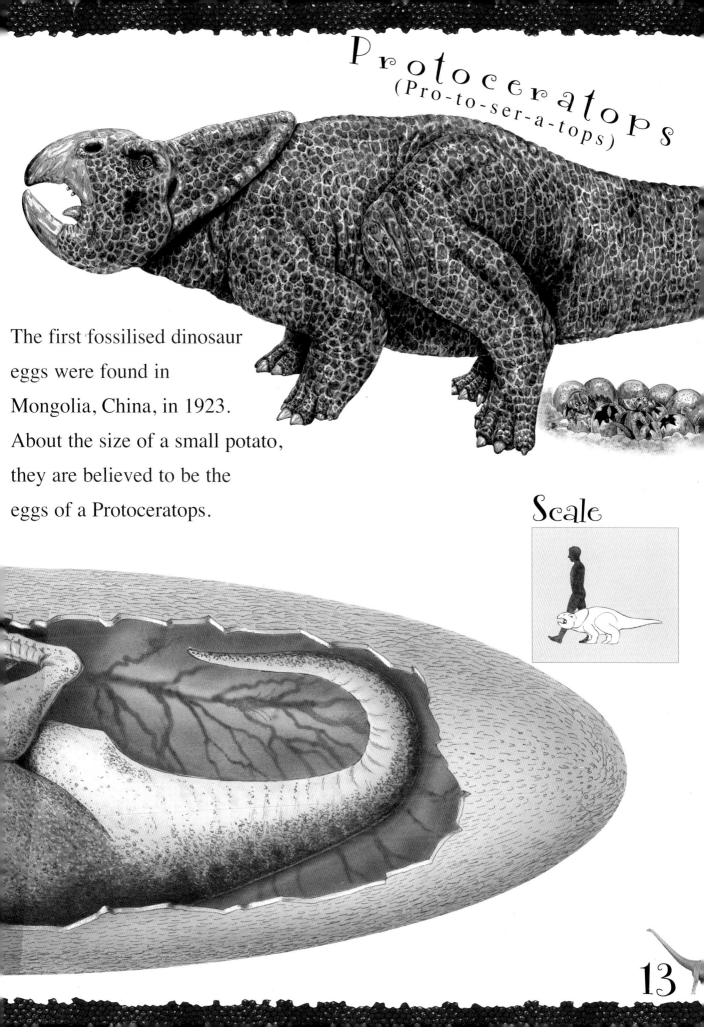

Protoceratops
(Pro-to-ser-a-tops)

The first fossilised dinosaur eggs were found in Mongolia, China, in 1923. About the size of a small potato, they are believed to be the eggs of a Protoceratops.

Scale

Were dinosaurs good mothers?

Like all animals, some dinosaurs were good mothers and others were not. The Maiasaura – which means 'good mother lizard' – seem to have looked after their babies well.

Maiasaura
(My-a-sore-a)

How large were dinosaur eggs?

The Maiasaura grouped their nests close together. The distance between them was about 7 metres – about the same length as a fully grown Maiasaura mother.

The Maiasaura laid batches of around 12 eggs. Each egg was about 12 centimetres long and rounded in shape. Despite the huge size of some dinosaurs, their babies were small – but they grew fast.

Large groups of Maiasaura, a herbivorous dinosaur, laid eggs in nest colonies.

Maiasaura mothers had to look out for hungry carnivores that might eat their young.

They may even have helped each other with babysitting. 15

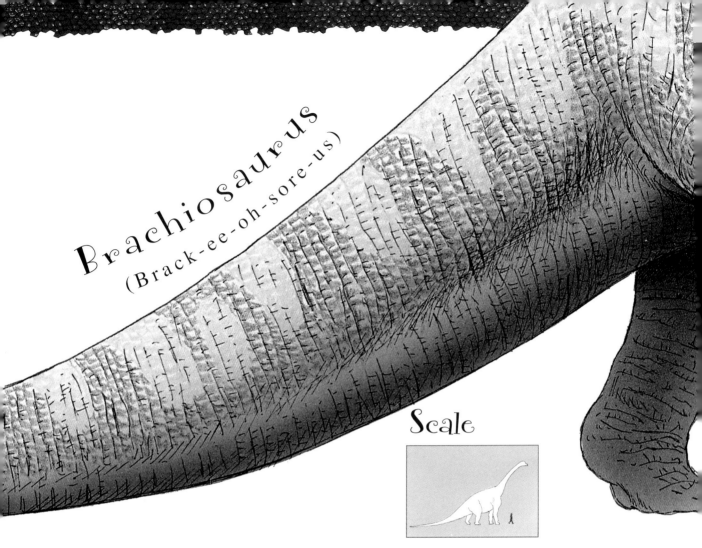

Brachiosaurus
(Brack-ee-oh-sore-us)

Scale

Was a dinosaur bigger than an elephant?

Yes, some dinosaurs were even bigger than buses. They were the biggest land-living animals on Earth.

Mamenchisaurus was a herbivore that was 22 metres long and 5 metres tall.

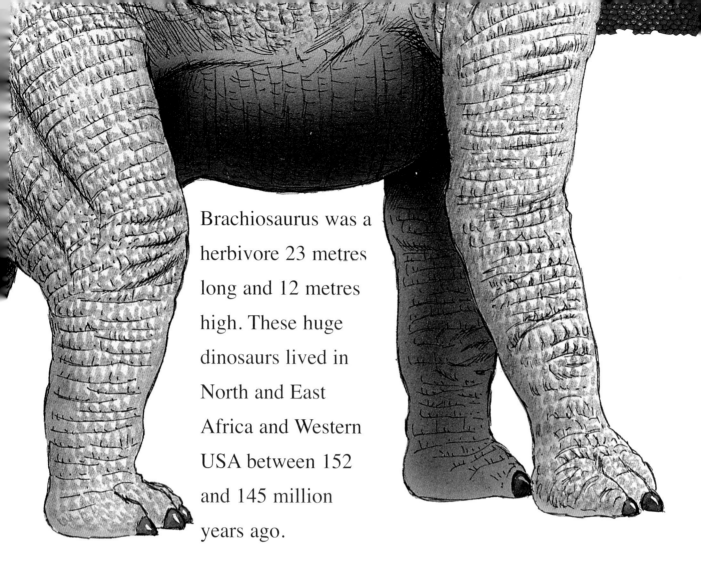

Brachiosaurus was a herbivore 23 metres long and 12 metres high. These huge dinosaurs lived in North and East Africa and Western USA between 152 and 145 million years ago.

Mamenchisaurus
(Ma-men-chee-sore-us)

It lived in China 145 million years ago.

True or False?
Dinosaurs ate trees.

? ? ?

Answers on page 31

?

Did dinosaurs swim?

Dinosaurs could not swim, but they probably did like to cool off in lakes or rivers. There were reptiles living at the same time as dinosaurs that could live in water, like **plesiosaurs** and **ichthyosaurs**.

Elasmosaurus
(E-laz-mo-sore-us)

The Elasmosaurus was the largest plesiosaur. It was not really a dinosaur, but a **Cretaceous** marine reptile with flippers.

Scale

Shonisaurus
(Shon-ee-sore-us)

True or False?

Dinosaurs lived in an age called 'Mesozoic', meaning 'middle life'.

Answers on page 31

Shonisaurus was the largest ichthyosaur, at 15 metres long. It lived in North America during the **Triassic** Period.

Did dinosaurs fly?

No, dinosaurs could not fly, but a group of reptiles called **pterosaurs** could fly. They had wings made of skin.

Pteranodon was one of the largest pterosaurs. Pteranodon fossils have been found in Europe and North America.

Fossils are the remains of animals or plants that died long ago. Over millions of years these remains have slowly turned into stone – they have **fossilised**.

Pteranodon
(Ter-an-o-don)

True or False?

Birds and reptiles are related.

? ? ? ?

Answers on page 31

Did dinosaurs have feathers?

Newly discovered fossils in China show that some small, early dinosaurs had feathers. The bones of these meat-eating dinosaurs were hollow and light, like birds' bones.

Scale

Large carnivores like Albertosaurus could probably run quickly for short distances. They may have reached speeds of 40 kilometres an hour.

Scale

Albertosaurus
(Al-bert-a-sore-us)

Could dinosaurs run?

Some dinosaurs did run. Scientists know this by measuring the distance between fossilised footprints. The space between the prints left by a running dinosaur is different from those of a walking dinosaur.

Footprints of an Albertosaurus running

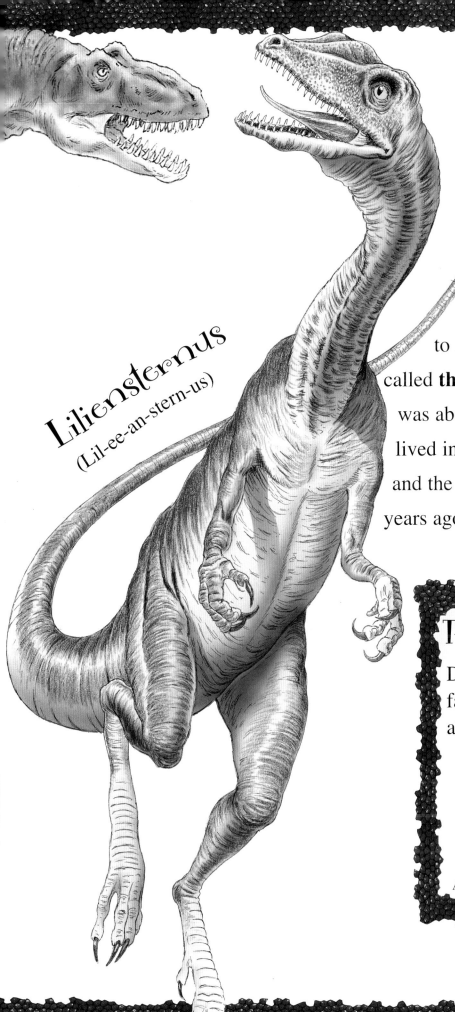

Lilicnsternus
(Lil-ee-an-stern-us)

Liliensternus and Albertosaurus belonged to a group of dinosaurs called **theropods**. Liliensternus was about 5 metres long and lived in Germany, New Mexico and the USA around 220 million years ago. It hunted larger reptiles.

True or False?

Dinosaurs could run faster than any animal alive today.

Answers on page 31

Did dinosaurs have bones?

Dinosaurs did have bones, and this is how scientists can study them. The soft parts of an animal's body rot away when it dies. Dinosaur fossils are almost always the remains of hard body parts like bones and teeth, as well as eggshells and gastroliths.

Crocodile

How is a crocodile useful for studying dinosaurs?

Scientists use their knowledge of existing reptiles, like crocodiles, to work out what kind of muscles and internal organs a dinosaur may have had.

How are dinosaur bones excavated?

Wet tissue paper is spread over the surface of the fossilised bone. Thick bandages are then soaked in plaster and spread over the tissue paper. When this has hardened, the fossil is carefully turned over and the other side is covered with paper and plaster. Then it can be lifted out.

True or False?

Tyrannosaurus rex was the scariest dinosaur of them all.

Answers on page 31

What killed the dinosaurs?

Dinosaurs, along with most of the swimming reptiles, suddenly disappeared forever. How did this happen? Many scientists believe that a giant meteor – a chunk of rock from outer space – smashed into the Earth. Dust from the impact would have clogged the skies, blocking out heat and light from the sun and plunging the planet into a cold darkness that may have lasted many months or even years.

How did the dinosaurs die?

Dust clouds spread across the planet.

Without warmth or light, all plants stop growing and die.

Plant-eaters slowly starve. The largest dinosaurs die first.

The meteor was about 15 km wide when it landed. It may have started out even bigger, but probably broke up in space.

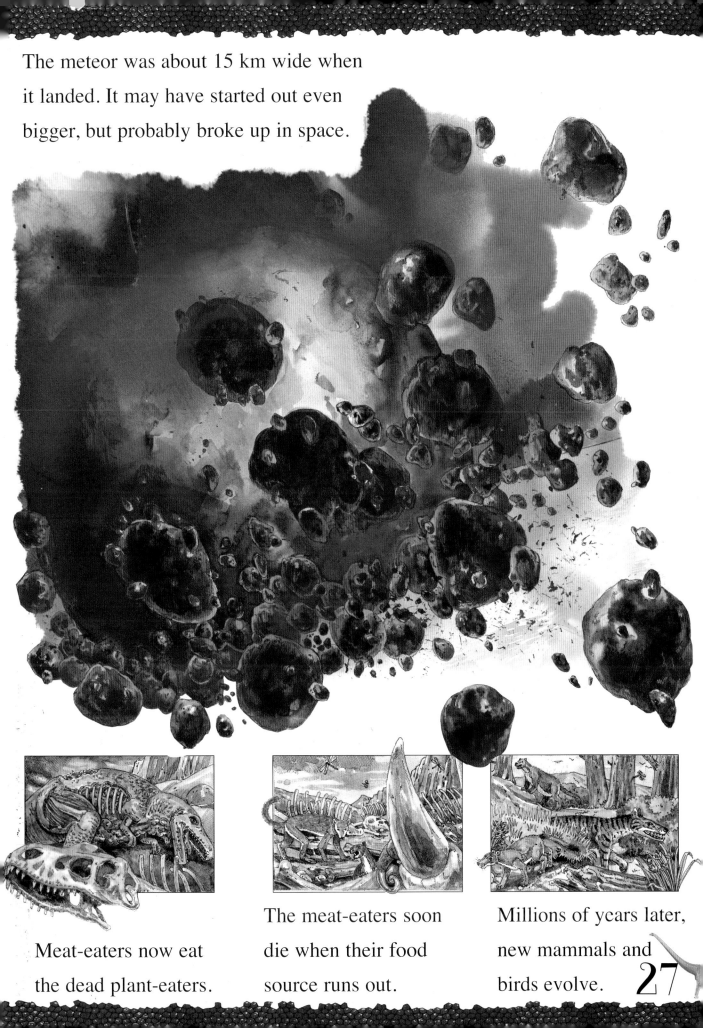

Meat-eaters now eat the dead plant-eaters.

The meat-eaters soon die when their food source runs out.

Millions of years later, new mammals and birds evolve.

27

How do we know about dinosaurs?

Scientists have dug up pieces of fossilised dinosaurs, and from these fragments they can work out what the dinosaur may have looked like. The size of a single bone can hold clues to how big the whole dinosaur may have been.

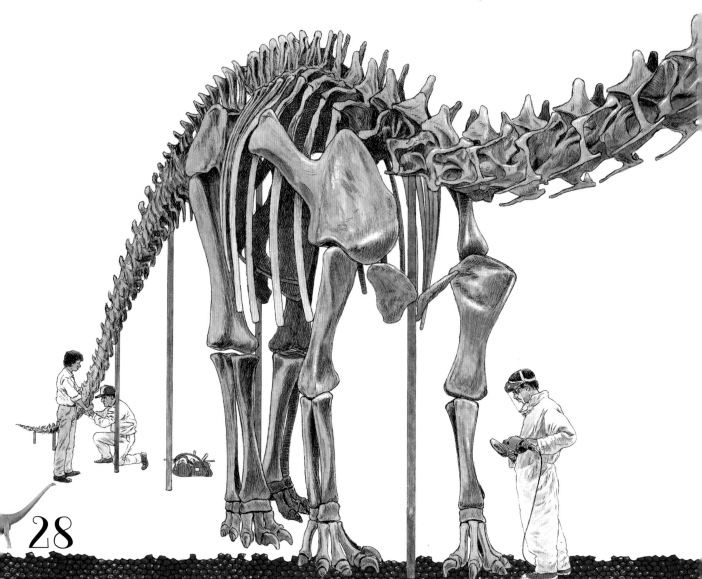

What can one dinosaur's tooth tell you?

One tooth might be enough to work out what the animal ate. Carnivores have sharp teeth, but herbivores have flat-topped teeth.

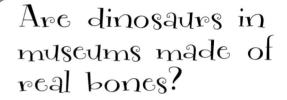

Are dinosaurs in museums made of real bones?

No, the skeletons you see in museums are exact copies of real dinosaur bones.

What happens to a fossilised bone?

Stones and debris are cleared away and the bones are covered in plaster.

At the museum the plaster is removed and a cast of the bone is made.

Artists work with scientists to plan how replica bones are put together.

Useful words

Carnivore A meat-eater.

Cretaceous The period from 146 to 65 million years ago. Dinosaurs disappeared at the end of this period.

Fossil The remains of a dead animal or plant, naturally preserved in the ground.

Gastrolith A stone swallowed by an animal to grind up its food.

Herbivore A plant-eater.

Ichthyosaur A fish-like swimming reptile.

Jurassic The period from 208 to 146 million years ago.

Omnivore A creature that eats both plants and meat.

Plesiosaur A long-necked swimming reptile.

Pterosaur A type of flying reptile from the time of the dinosaurs.

Theropod A type of dinosaur that walked or ran on two legs.

Triassic The period from 245 to 208 million years ago.

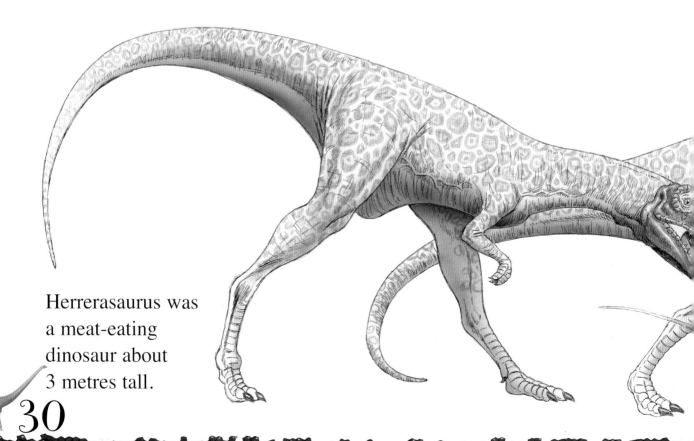

Herrerasaurus was a meat-eating dinosaur about 3 metres tall.

Answers

Page 7 TRUE! Yes, there were more than 700 different types of dinosaur, including meat-eaters (carnivores) like Tyrannosaurus rex and plant-eaters (herbivores) like Stegosaurus.

Page 8 TRUE! Yes, the teeth of Tyrannosaurus rex had saw-like edges, perfect for slicing through meat. The teeth were 20 cm long. Only a small part would be visible above the gum.

Page 10 TRUE! Yes, the word 'dinosaur' means 'terrible lizard' in Greek.

Page 17 TRUE! Yes, scientists who have studied fossilised droppings have found that they contain a lot of wood fibres from trees. It seems that at least some herbivorous dinosaurs did eat very tough wood.

Page 19 TRUE! Yes, dinosaurs lived in a time called Mesozoic, and this means 'middle life' in Greek.

Page 21 TRUE! Yes, birds and reptiles are closely related. A fossil animal called Archaeopteryx had feathers like a bird, as well as the teeth, claws and tail of a dinosaur.

Page 23 FALSE! No, the fastest dinosaurs are thought to have been the ornithomimids, who may have been able to reach speeds of around 45 km/h. Today's cheetah can reach 100 km/h.

Page 25 TRUE! Yes, Tyrannosaurus, taller than a double-decker bus and about 14 metres long, must have been truly fearsome – though scientists now think some other carnivores may have been even bigger!

Roar!

Herrerasaurus
(Heh-rare-a-sore-us)

Eoraptor
(Ee-oh-rap-tor)

Index

(Illustrations are shown in **bold type**.)